Benefits of the Book

If you want your child to overcome the fear of Public Speaking and enjoy it, this book is for you. People fear Public Speaking due to lack of knowledge and practise. It addresses both these points. This book will help your child in:
a. Increasing confidence
b. Doing well in elocution competitions
c. Increasing participation in social events – dance, singing, etc.
d. Better performance in the school – speaking in front of the class, recitation and answering the questions asked by the teachers.

How to use the Book

This book is based on an interesting story of 2 children. You will meet them and also experience their real life situations - at home, school and other places. So, become familiar with them. Read the chapters in the given sequence. Exercises given at the end of every chapter should be done alongwith the chapter for an amazing learning experience.

Exercises include speaking on various topics. For better learning, ensure that you do this with a group - parents, friends, siblings, relatives, etc. Record the videos of your speech and use it for improvement.

At the end of every chapter you will find some stars. You have to earn them. This can be done by completing the exercises and using what you learn from every chapter. After you complete all the chapters and the exercises, you will get a certificate.

Let's hear what experts have to say...

Your book is superb! It will be a great help to all the aspiring speakers.

Ms. Sudha Menon, Principal, North Point ICSE School, Navi Mumbai

The "Making Champs" book on Public Speaking focusses on developing confidence in children. The pragmatic and systematic approach ensures progress.
Ms. Anahita Devitre, Former Principal, J. B. Petit High School, Mumbai

I would highly recommend this excellent book on Public Speaking for children! They have brought this very essential subject alive in a very interactive format which I am sure young growing minds will really enjoy engaging with.
Anand Tendolkar, Founder CEO and Happiness Coach, Energy Centre

Our education system only focuses on academics and there is a crying need for programmes for Personality Development. "Making Champs" has initiated steps in that direction and this book is one more such positive step.
Moiz Miyajiwala, Hon. Treasurer, Anjuman-I-Islam & Ex- CFO, Voltas Ltd.

From the Authors' Desk............

Public Speaking is an essential skill and a core aspect of our personality.

Our belief is that Public Speaking is an acquired skill i.e. whoever works at it, can improve it. However, it is a difficult art. Therefore, all children should get inputs and opportunities at an early stage. This book is an attempt to reach out to more children and parents so that we can share with them the techniques for improving Public Speaking in a simple and a fun way.
Happy Learning!

Mili Pahade Chartered Accountant Co-Founder, Making Champs

Prasanna Pahade   B.E, PGDM (IIM Calcutta) Co-Founder, Making Champs

Oct 22, 2015
Navi Mumbai, India

Contents

Remember to keep an eye for the following in all chapters:

a. Learning Videos (Given as hyperlinks)

b. Do you know (Interesting things related to the topic)

c. Mantra (Action items related to the topic)

d. Stars for the chapter (Students can record the stars based on the logic – completing the home assignments and using the learnings)

**Note: This book addresses both the genders. Her or she has been used for simplicity.*

1.Public Speaking

Hello Champs!

You will be learning various skills through a story. Let us meet the Verma family – the main characters in our story.

Verma family has recently shifted from Pune to Navi Mumbai. Rajan and Sonal have also changed their school. As they settle down, their parents enrol them with Vikas Uncle, who works with school children for developing their personality.

Vikas Uncle starts his class with the topic of Public Speaking.

Vikas Uncle

Mantra for the Champ

Becoming good in Public Speaking is an effective way of developing your personality.

Vikas Uncle: Children, what is Public Speaking?

Rajan: Uncle, Public Speaking is speaking to a group.

Sonal: Like our Principal.

Vikas Uncle: Correct. Public speaking is speaking to a group of people. E.g. teacher in a class, student speaking in the assembly, or the host of a program.

Public Speaking is essential for everyone.

Vikas Uncle: Now tell me, where is Public Speaking required?

Rajan: School competitions.

Rajan: Building functions.

Boy: In a party.

Vikas Uncle: Yes, you all are correct. As students, you would be required to speak in public at many places like recitation in the class, speaking in the assembly, elocution competition, hosting a party, speaking to the family, speech on Independence Day, etc.

Do you know?
Glossophobia – fear of Public Speaking, is the most common phobia. It is in the top three fears across the world.

Let me tell you, the formula for good Public Speaking:
CCDPP

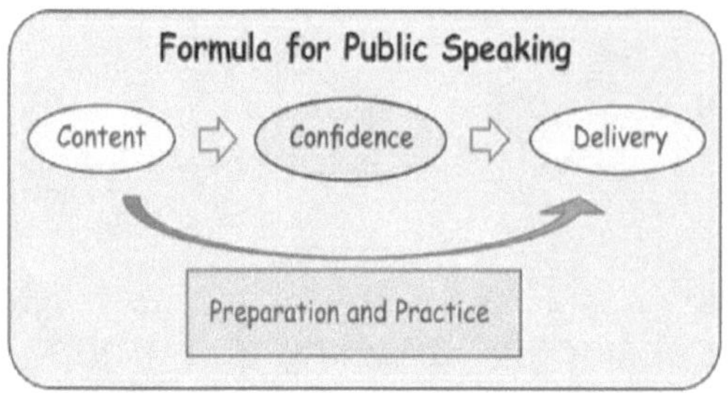

Mantra for the Champ

Shortform or acronym helps to improve memory.So, next time you have to speak in your class, remember CCDPP.

C	C	D	P & P
Content	**Confidence**	**Delivery**	**Preparation & Practice**
What you say (the matter)	Belief that you will be successful	How you speak	The efforts to ensure perfect delivery

Vikas Uncle: Remember this whenever you have to speak in public. Complete your home assignment and we will discuss more about Public Speaking in the next class.

Rajan and Sonal are very happy to learn this new skill from Vikas Uncle. They think that this will make them smarter than others.

Exercises

1. Which are the Public Speaking situations from the list given below:

a. Speaking with your bench partner in the recess.

b. Story telling competition in your society in Ganeshotsav.

c. News reading in the assembly.

d. Speaking with your parents at the dinner table.

e. Sharing a joke at a birthday party.

f. Poem recitation in the class.

2. Remember the best Public Speaking experience you had. Describe it.

Practise

Speaking Assignment: Speak as per the instructions given below and record the video of the same.

a. Narrate a story to your friends.

b. Describe a day in your school to your parents.

c. Prepare and speak on : My best birthday party.

d. Prepare and speak on : The most interesting event during the last week.

Note down the stars achieved:
Green Stars – for using the learnings
Red Stars- for completing the exercise

2. Delivery: How you Speak

Rajan and Sonal are very happy that they joined Vikas Uncle's class. They tell their parents excitedly about what they learnt in the first few classes.

Let's see what is happening in Vikas Uncle's class.

Vikas Uncle: You remember the formula CCDPP? Out of these 5 things, tell me what is the first thing your listeners would notice?

Rajan: Confidence. They will immediately know if I am nervous or confident.

Sonal: Delivery. Because it is about how we speak.

Vikas Uncle: Yes, it is delivery. Listeners would observe this and hence it is very important to get this right. Let us understand more about it.

You know about pizza delivery – The pizza shop takes care that the pizza is baked as per the order, packed in a proper box, then the delivery boy takes the pizza and delivers it to your home.

In the same way, you have to speak in such a way that your content (matter) is transferred properly to the listeners so that they understand it. This is called Delivery in speaking.

Delivery - how you speak includes:

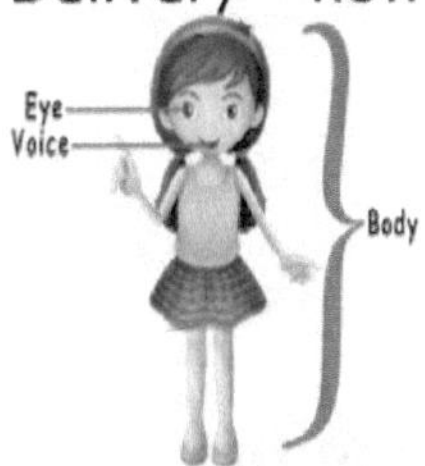

1. Eye Contact – look into the eyes of the listeners
2. Voice – use the right voice to make it interesting for the listeners
3. Body Language – use your body effectively
4. Avoid Mannerisms – avoid repeated use of certain words or actions

Delivery is the most visible part of speaking. We like speakers such as Narendra Modi, Amitabh Bachchan as they use delivery very effectively. You can watch some sample videos.

Video: https://goo.gl/l8sQu8
Video: https://goo.gl/F2tJ0d
Video: https://goo.gl/XeWxlj

Mantra for the Champ
How you speak (delivery) is as important as what you speak (content). Use this tip to make your speech more interesting.

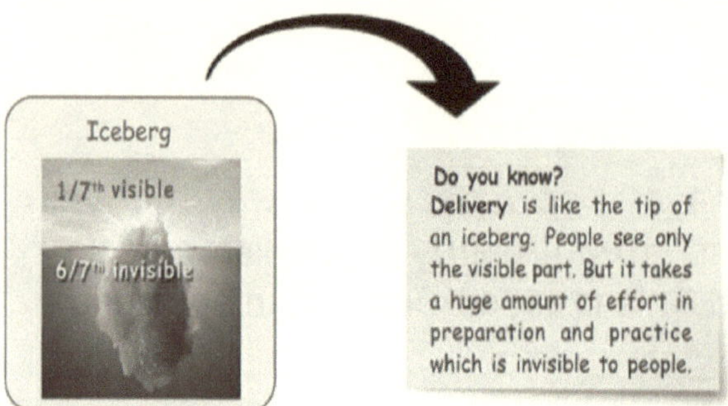

Vikas Uncle: We will study delivery in great detail in the next few weeks. Till that time, keep using the learnings.
Exercises

1. Observe the speakers around you carefully at school, home, TV, etc.
a. Select a speaker whose speech you liked. Write down what did you like about his speech.
b. Select a speaker whose speech you did not like. Write down what did you not like about his speech.
2. Speak on a topic, get it recorded and watch the video. Please note what you <u>liked </u>about the way you have spoken and what do you think <u>needs to be improved</u>.
a. Things I liked about my speech
b. Things I need to improve in my speech
Practise
Tell stories to your parents and friends in an interesting way. Record them on the smart phone and observe your delivery.
Note down the stars achieved:
Green Stars – for using the learnings
Red Stars- for completing the exercise

3. Eye Contact

Rajan & Sonal are very excited with the kind of home assignments they are getting at Vikas Uncle's class; watching videos, TV and noting down their observations. This is very different from their regular school homework.

Mr. Verma: Rajan, Sonal, why are you watching all these videos?

Rajan: This is our assignment. We have to note down what is good and what needs to be better in the delivery of the speech.

In Vikas Uncle's class, they continue the journey of knowing more about delivery.

Vikas Uncle: Today, we will learn about Eye Contact.

<u>Eye Contact is looking into the eyes of the listeners.</u>

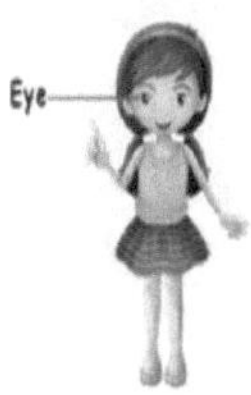

Sonal: Why is it required?

Vikas Uncle: While speaking in public, you can connect with the listeners by using Eye Contact. When you make eye contact with the listeners, they feel that you are personally speaking to them. This also helps the listeners to be more attentive.

Rajan: Yes Uncle, when teacher makes eye contact with me, I become very attentive.

Mantra for the Champ
To address nervousness, start making eye contact with people who appear friendly.

SUCCESS TIPS

1. You have to cover the entire group by making eye contact. This can be done by starting from one direction and then slowly turning to the others in the audience.

2. Maintain eye contact for 1- 2 seconds and then move to others.

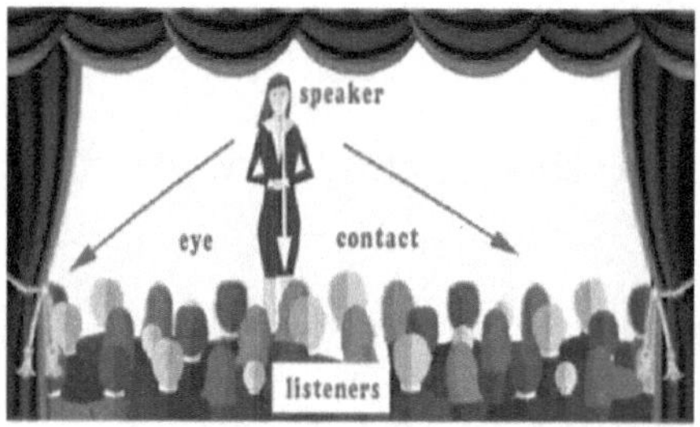

Mantra for the Champ
If there are a less number of listeners you can make eye contact with each one of them. But if the listeners are more, you can cover them, group by group.

Watch the following video to get an idea of how it is done:

Video - Success tips https://goo.gl/xvL2Cr

THINGS TO AVOID

1. Looking up or down at the ceiling, walls, floor or mike.

2. Only looking towards the camera or the chief guest or an important person.

3. Rapid movements of the head.

4. Moving only the eye balls.

Watch the following video for better understanding:

Video - Things to avoid https://goo.gl/QhRKuY

Do you know?
When you make eye contact with the listeners, they respond with a nod, smile, and other expressions.

Mantra for the Champ
Make eye contact whenever you speak to anyone. This will help you in Public Speaking.

Exercises

1. Observe people speaking to public - TV, video or in person and note:

a. People who make good eye contact

b. People who do not make good eye contact

2. Watch this video and answer the quiz:
http://zapt.io/tsqwa6ng

3. Watch your own videos recorded earlier. Assess the effectiveness of your eye contact? (Select the right option)

Coverage: Only part / Everyone

Maintain: 1-2 seconds / Fast

Movement: Neck / Only eyeballs

Distractions: Ceiling, mike, others / None

Practise

Be conscious that you have to make eye contact whenever you are speaking. Note down instances when you made eye contact.

Note down the stars achieved:
Green Stars – for using the learnings
Red Stars- for completing the exercise

4. Voice

Let's see what is happening in the Verma family.

Rajan: Mom, Vikas uncle has asked us to see Amitabh's video. His voice is so good.

Mrs. Verma: I'm glad to know that Vikas Uncle is telling you all these things.

Do you know?
a. Good speakers take care of their voice. Before any speaking event they avoid icecream, cold drinks or oily food.
b. For clearing your voice before the speaking event – drink hot water or gargle with warm salt water.

In Vikas Uncle's class:

Vikas Uncle: We have learnt about eye contact. Let us discuss why Voice is important.

Sonal: Uncle, even if we don't want to be singer, do we need to have a good voice?

Vikas Uncle: Listeners should be able to hear and understand your speech. Therefore, Voice is important.

Rajan: I love to hear Jeeturaj on Radio Mirchi and even Kapil Sharma.

Vikas Uncle: All of us like to listen to good speakers. They use their voice effectively to make the speech interesting. Let us understand what makes our voice effective.

Mantra for the Champ
Drink a glass of water before your speech for better voice.

Essentials of effective voice are:

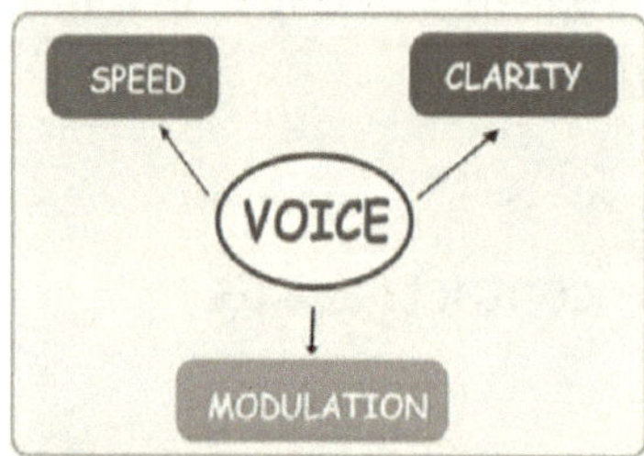

SUCCESS TIPS:

1. Clarity : The voice should be audible (appropriately loud).Pronunciations should be clear.

2. Speed: Proper speed (neither too fast nor too slow).

3. Modulation: Some words/ sentences to be emphasized in a high or low voice to make the speech interesting.

THINGS TO AVOID:

1. Clarity: Unclear pronunciations and inaudible voice.

2. Speed: Fast speed or slow speed.

3. Modulation: Monotonous/ expressionless/ dull voice.

Check this video to understand each of the above elements of voice:

Learning video – Voice https://goo.gl/aBjQFV

Vikas Uncle: From now on, be conscious about how you speak and pay attention to your voice.

Mantra for the Champ
Play tongue twisters to improve your voice clarity.

Do you know?
The way you modulate voice can change the meaning of what you are saying. Watch this funny video from a Hindi movie to understand this. https://goo.gl/O9VYNP

Mantra for the Champ
Pausing at the punctuation marks makes the speech interesting. It also gives the time to breathe. If it is a full stop, count 1-2-3 in your mind, if it is a comma, count 1-2 while practising.

Exercises

1. Listen some speeches and make a note of the following based on the voice of the speaker:

Effective voice: Yes / No

2. Listen to the audio in the clips below and answer the quiz.

http://zapt.io/tct3b32m

http://zapt.io/t856gecx

3. Listen to your own voice from the speeches recorded earlier. Is your voice clear, at the right speed & modulated?

4. Play the game of these tongue twisters with your friends/ family. The one who speaks for the highest number, at a fast pace, without fumbling will be the winner.

a. Red Blood Blue Blood

b. Red Lorry Yellow Lorry

c. Busy Buzzing Bumble Bees

d. Kaccha Papad Pakka Papad

Practise

Speak the following lines – clearly, at the right speed and with modulation. Record them and listen to yourself.

1. Wow, this looks very beautiful!

2. No, I don't want to drink milk now.

3. Did you get this from Macdonalds?

Note down the stars achieved:
Green Stars – for using the learnings
Red Stars- for completing the exercise

5. Body Language

Vikas Uncle: Rajan, are you not feeling well?
Rajan: Yes Uncle. But how did you know? I didn't tell anyone.
Vikas Uncle: You are appearing very dull and so I asked you.
That brings me to another important part of delivery - **Body Language**.

<u>When you speak, your body conveys the message along with your words e.g. facial expressions, movements of your hands, legs. This is called Body Language.</u>

Vikas Uncle: You can make your speech interesting by using the correct body language to support the words. Elements of Body Language are:
1. Facial Expressions - The message conveyed by our face
2. Posture – The way we stand
3. Gestures - The use of hands (and sometimes legs)

Do you know?
You cannot be fully dressed without a smile.

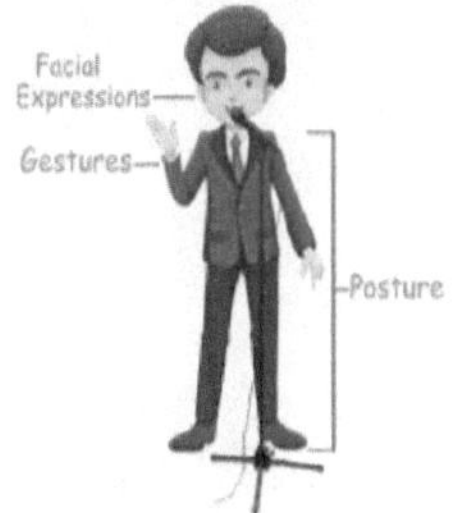

Vikas Uncle: Let us look at each one of them in detail.

Facial Expressions: It helps to start with a smile on your face. Later, you can change the expressions according to what you say.

Let's see below how our face can convey different feelings.
You can make use of these and other expressions while you
are speaking.

Watch the following video to understand the impact of facial
expressions:
Learning video: https://goo.gl/DrXxTA

Posture: Your posture indicates your confidence. You should
be in a comfortable posture. Remember, how the news
readers or the TV anchors stand – feet slightly apart and
hands in front.

Do you know?
Generally, the bad posture is uncomfortable for your body.

Given below are images of some postures.

Watch the following video to know the correct posture:
Learning video: https://goo.gl/Uv8ORd

Gestures: You can make a dramatic impact in your speech

when you use gestures to support your words e.g. commonly used gestures would be for:

1. Size – small/ large

2. Height – short/ tall

 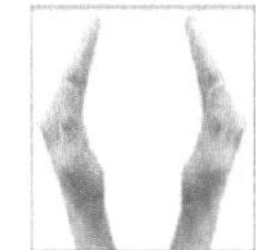

3. Numbers - 1, 2, 3

4. Pointing – at yourself, at listeners or the world in general

And there are many more....check some of them below :

Mantra for the Champ
Excessive gestures are distracting for the listeners. Use them selectively.

Watch the following video to know the importance of gestures:
Learning video: https://goo.gl/ku8yZj

Sonal: Uncle, there are so many things to remember – Eye Contact, Voice and now Body Language.

Rajan: I never imagined that Public Speaking will involve so many things.

Vikas Uncle: That is the reason why Public Speaking is

complex. But now you have learnt all these skills. Keep on practising and later on, you will be able to do it naturally.

Rajan: Yes. I am going to use all that I am learning – at home as well as in the school.

Do you know?
Communication = 20% words + 80% body language.Generally, people believe in body language more than the words.

Mantra for the Champ
Use friendly body language to make your communication effective and acceptable.

Exercises

1. Observe your parents carefully when they are speaking with you. Make a list of different expressions they use.

2. Observe people around you. Note down who used good posture and who did not use good posture while speaking.

3. Watch the video clip given below and answer the quiz: http://zapt.io/tswy5ge4

4. Observe your earlier video and make a note of the following:

a. I used expression for _______________________________

b. I could have used expression for

____

c. I used gesture for ________________________________

d. I could have used gesture for ____________________

(E.g. I used the expression for sad. I could have used expression for surprise. I used gesture for myself and I could have used gesture for large.)

Practise

1. Speak the following lines with appropriate expressions and voice, video record it and observe how you appear.

a. I am feeling tired at the end of such a hectic day in school.

b. Why did you take my pen without asking me?

c. Wow, what a beautiful dress!

2. Speak the following lines with appropriate gestures, video record it and see how you appear.

a. The sound was coming from the small hole in the shoe box.

b. I request all of you to plant more trees.

c. In the summer vacation, I went to 3 places.

Note down the stars achieved:
Green Stars – for using the learnings
Red Stars- for completing the exercise

6. Mannerisms

Rajan: Uncle, yesterday a teacher came to our school for a trial class. She is very fond of the word 'basically'.

Vikas Uncle: Is it? How did you notice it?

Rajan: I don't know. It just caught my attention. Then I started counting. She said "basically" 8-10 times!

Vikas Uncle: Good you spotted that. These are called Mannerisms.

Mannerisms mean repeating words or actions, unconsciously.

Sonal: Why does someone have mannerisms?

Vikas Uncle: Often, the person is not conscious about it therefore this happens. It also indicates nervousness and lack of practise.

Do you know?
Manners and Mannerisms are different.Manners are good way of behaving e.g.saying "please", "thank you", etc.Mannerisms are actions that happen unconsciously and can irritate others.

Commonly found mannerisms are:

1. Blinking (impacts eye contact)

2. Using filler words - like, er, you see, basically, umm, actually, of course, I know, you know, etc. or repeating the words or part of the sentence (impacts voice)

3. Playing with clothes, pen, mike, table, etc. or scratching, nail biting, moving constantly, etc. (impacts body language)

Watch this video to know how you appear if you have mannerisms:
Learning video: https://goo.gl/pXc8N5

Mannerisms have to be avoided. This can be done by more practise and following the rules of good Eye Contact, Voice and Body Language.

Mantra for the Champ

When you practise your speech in front of listeners, get feedback from them. If you have any mannerisms, consciously work on removing them.

Exercises

1. Watch your earlier video and list if you have any mannerisms.

2. Observe people around you and list if they have any mannerisms.

3. Watch the video below and spot the mannerisms.

Practise

1. Tell a story in front of your family members. Get feedback from them whether you have any mannerisms. Note them down.

Note down the stars achieved:
Green Stars – for using the learnings
Red Stars- for completing the exercise

7. Confidence

Sonal: Rajan, I am nervous about the elocution competition. The last time I participated, I had forgotten part of my speech.

Rajan: I also feel very nervous on the stage. Let us ask Vikas Uncle how to deal with it

Rajan and Sonal ask this question to Vikas Uncle.

Mantra for the Champ
Many times, the speaker fears about people criticising or laughing at him. Think positive and do your best.

Vikas Uncle: Sonal, tell us why you could not remember your speech?
Sonal: My Mom added a paragraph at the last moment. Therefore I could not practise much.
Rajan: I had practised well, but I kept thinking that my friend Soham was going to do better than me.
Vikas Uncle: Ok. Let us learn how to increase self confidence.
Mantra for the Champ
Using positive body language increases confidence.

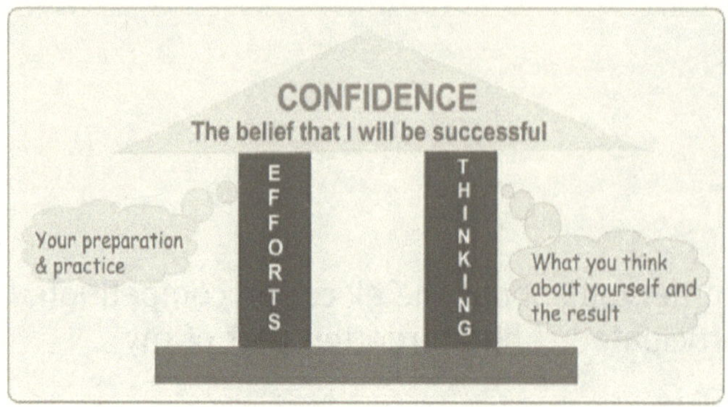

Vikas Uncle: Effort is very important. We will study later how to prepare and practise for the speech. Let's focus on thinking.

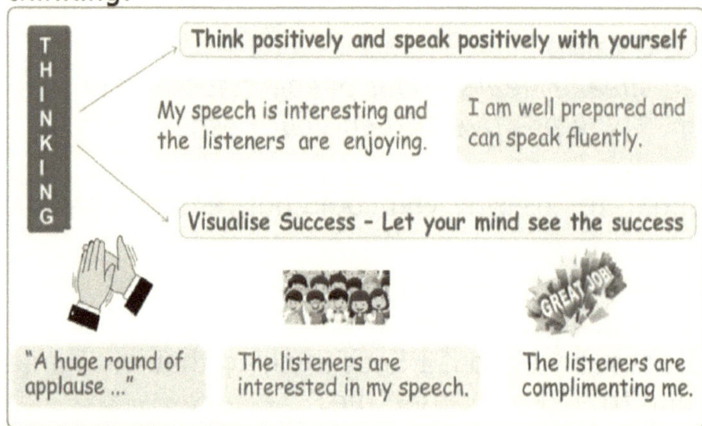

Do you know?
Confidence is important for overcoming Glossophobia and it is based on our self -belief. In the absence of confidence, no technique can work.

Do you know?
Inspite of visualising success, one may make mistakes. But, confident people learn from their failure and try again.

Remember to match your efforts and thinking.

Exercises

1. Observe speakers around you. Classify them as under:

a. Confident speakers

b. Non-confident speakers

2. Watch your earlier video and assess your confidence (Select the right option).

a. Very Confident

b. Confident

c. Nervous

d. Very Nervous

3. State if the statements given below would help in increasing your confidence (Yes/ No). If "No", then write the correct statement.

a. I am well prepared for the elocution competition.

b. I feel that I am going to forget my speech.

c. I can see my name on the 1st prize certificate.

Practise

I used the techniques for increasing confidence as below:

Speaking Situation	Positive Talk	Visualising Success
a.		
b.		

Note down the stars achieved:
Green Stars – for using the learnings
Red Stars- for completing the exercise

8. Selecting the Content

Rajan had to speak on "My Favourite Singer". He worked hard and spoke well, but he did not win the prize. He was a bit disappointed. He asks Vikas Uncle about this.

Rajan: Uncle, I followed all the body language rules. But my speech was not selected.

Vikas Uncle: Good speech is not only about good body language. Content is also important. So tell me what is content?

Sonal: It is the matter - What we speak.

Do you know?
Good content is the heart of Public Speaking. The audience will get bored if the content is not interesting.

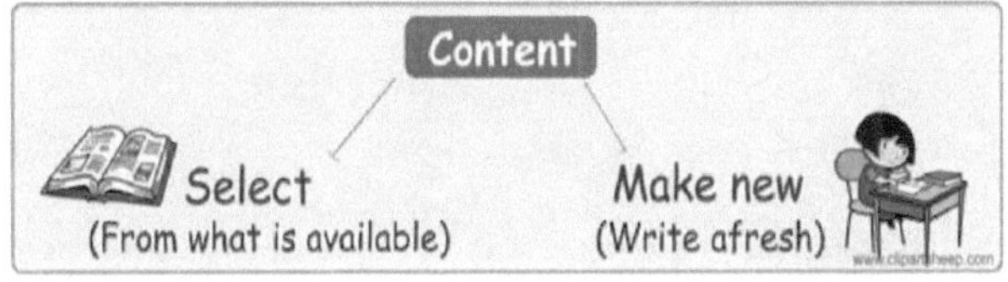

Vikas Uncle: More often you would select the content. You need to ensure that your content is interesting.

Good content should make the audience think and stir their emotions (happy, sad, etc.)

Sonal: How do we select good content?

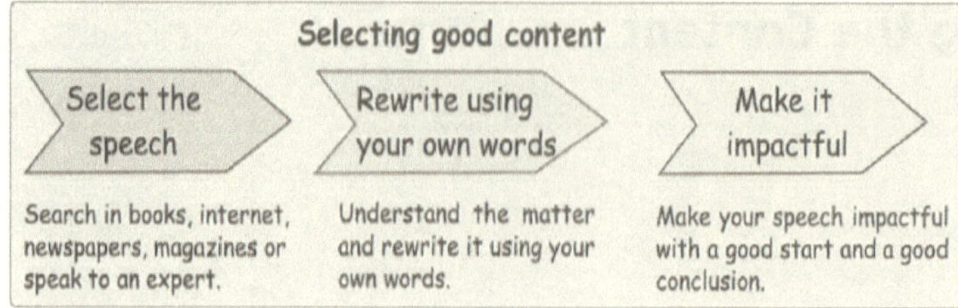

Mantra For the Champ

If you have ready to use content, you can focus more on improving delivery.

Good Start:

1. A question to the audience

2. A proverb or a famous quote

3. Current news or an unusual fact

4. A personal experience

5. A song or a poem

Good Conclusion:

1. A question to the audience

2. A song or a poem or a quote

3. A dramatic or an optimistic future

4. An action item for the audience

5. An overview for a long speech

Watch the following video to see examples:

Learning video - Good start and conclusion:
https://goo.gl/ZSzdXp

Vikas Uncle: Rajan, tell us how did you start your speech?

Vikas Uncle: Here your content is fine. But there should be something else which will make the start interesting/ catchy.

Sonal: Uncle, so how Rajan should have started or ended his speech?

START

"Nagada, nagada, nagada bajaa", who is the singer? Any guess? Yes, you guessed right, Sonu Nigam. I will speak about My Favourite Singer Sonu Nigam.

CONCLUSION

I wish my favourite singer is a guest at our building in the near future or I would love to get a chance to be a playback singer in one of his albums………

Do you know?
The audience develops an impression in the first 30 seconds of the speech. Hence, an attention grabbing start is essential.

Rajan: Now, I know. I will do better next time.

Exercises

1. You have to speak on the topic Trees are our Best Friends. How will you start your speech to grab the attention of the audience?

2. You have to speak on the topic My Favourite

Teacher. How will you conclude your speech with an impact?

3. This is the speech available on the internet. Modify it and write it in your notebook.

Remember: Use your own words and make an impactful start and conclusion.

The Peacock

Our national bird is the peacock. I love the peacock as it is a very beautiful bird.

The colour of the peacock is dark blue. It has colourful feathers and a soft blue, graceful neck. It has a bright shining tail. The female peacock is called a peahen and it does not have all these attractive features.

The peacock eats fruits, seeds, grains, worms and insects. It is a great enemy of snakes. The peacock can fly but not to great distances. The peacock is afraid of tigers and foxes.

In the past, the peacock used to be a pet of rich people. Its feathers are very costly. According to Hindus, the peacock is a sacred bird. It is.a vehicle of God Karthikeya.

I love the peacock very much.

Note down the stars achieved:

9. Preparation and Practice

Mr. & Mrs. Verma saw some of the videos of Rajan and Sonal speaking in Vikas Uncle's class. They were happy with the progress made by Rajan and Sonal.

In Vikas Uncle's class:

Rajan: Uncle, we have done CCD from the CCDPP. When are we going to start with PP?

Vikas Uncle: Ok! So you people are eager to learn new things.

Sonal: Actually, he has a competition in school and he wants to know more about Preparation & Practice.

Vikas Uncle: Ok. Today we are going to learn about Preparation & Practice.

Mantra for the Champ

Enjoy your performance! If you enjoy it, only then will your audience enjoy it.

Preparation means to get ready for an event.

Actress doing make-up before the show

Cricketers playing football before the tournament

Chess player in the gym for physical fitness

Sonal: But Uncle, we are studying Public Speaking. Why do we need all these examples?

Do you know?
In addition to preparation for the specific skill, we have to prepare for overall fitness.

Preparation for Public Speaking

Vikas Uncle: We need to get ready for Public Speaking. All these examples tell us that preparation is required in any type of skill.

In Public Speaking, Preparation happens at 3 levels:

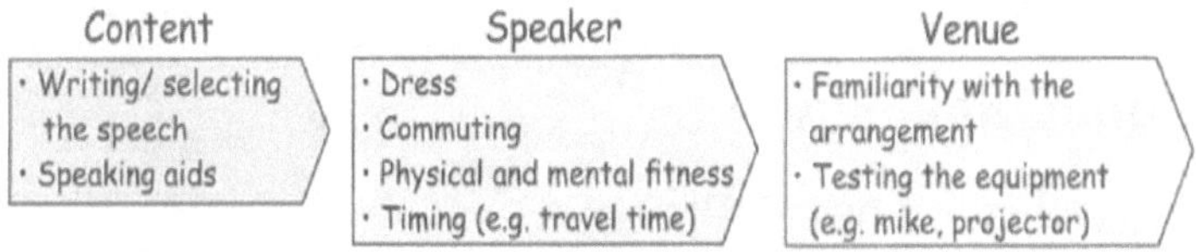

Sonal: I have one problem. I forget my speech very often.

Vikas Uncle: There is a way to handle this. You don't have to learn by heart your speech word by word. Focus on the essence.

Mantra for the Champ
Proper attire creates an impact on the audience. So, dress appropriately for the occasion.

There are 2 situations based on speaking aids - where you can use them (meeting, family and school function) and where you cannot (exams, competitions)

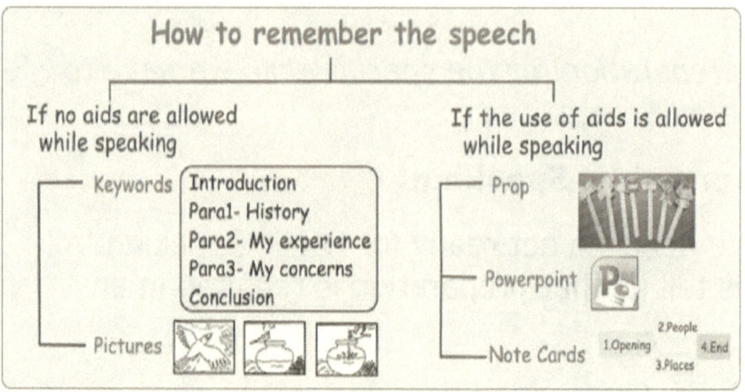

Video - How to remember the speech https://goo.gl/T2flDI

Practise for Public Speaking

Vikas Uncle: So, tell me what is Practise?

Rajan: I know - Practice makes a man perfect.

Do you know?
There is no substitute to hard work and practice. All good performers have a special skill – the ability to put in rigorous practice.

Practise means to do something again and again in order to become better at it.

Vikas Uncle: This is true in sports, dance, music and all other skills including Public Speaking. Practise is required not for just getting it right once, it is essential for getting it right every time we do it.

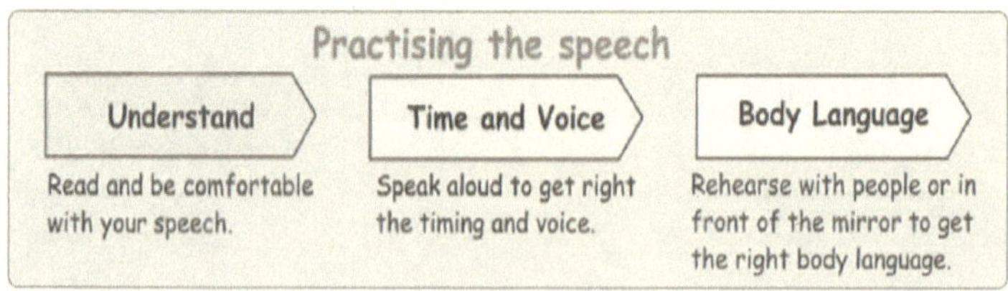

Do you know?
Good speech without speaking aid requires atleast 8 to 10 rounds of rehearsals.

Mantra for the Champ
Manage your time to reach the venue at least 10-15 minutes before the schedule to become familiar with the place.

Exercises

1. For your speaking performance, make a note of following steps.
a. How did you prepare?
Content:
Speaker:
Venue:

b. How did you practise?
Understand:
Time and Voice:
Body Language:

2. How was your speech after following the steps in preparation and practice as compared to your earlier experiences?
Note down the stars achieved:
Green Stars – for using the learnings
Red Stars- for completing the exercise

EPILOGUE

Rajan & Sonal learnt about Public Speaking from Vikas Uncle. They used the learnings in the school and various other social events. Both of them did well in the Interhouse elocution competition. Sonal got a prize in the story telling competition in their society.

Their significant achievement was that, both of them hosted a cultural evening in their society.

Most important learning for them was: **"Use it or Lose it"**.

Mr. and Mrs. Verma were very happy with the progress they saw with Rajan and Sonal.

Therefore they continued using what they had learnt from Vikas Uncle.

Mr. and Mrs. Verma were very happy with the progress they saw with Rajan and Sonal. They also played a helping role by having a weekly conversation on how they were using the learnings. Exciting part for Rajan and Sonal was receiving stars from their parents if they did well and used the learnings.

Making Champs is a Personality, EQ and IQ development program for children.

<u>***Skills covered:***</u>

Communication

Planning

Team Work

Managing Emotions

Critical Thinking